Video Games and Society

Video Games and Youth

Video Games
and Youth

Andrea C. Nakaya

ReferencePoint
Press®

San Diego, CA

© 2015 ReferencePoint Press, Inc.
Printed in the United States

For more information, contact:
ReferencePoint Press, Inc.
PO Box 27779
San Diego, CA 92198
www. ReferencePointPress.com

LIBRARY OF CONGRESS CATALOGING-IN-PUBLICATION DATA

Nakaya, Andrea C., 1976-
  Video games and youth / by Andrea C. Nakaya.
      pages cm. — (Video games and society)
  Audience: Grade 9 to 12.
  Includes bibliographical references and index.
  ISBN-13: 978-1-60152-750-9 (hardback)
  ISBN-10: 1-60152-750-0 (hardback)
  1. Video games and children--Juvenile literature. I. Title.
  HQ784.V53N35 2015
  794.8083—dc23
                                                           2014010450

Contents

A Favorite Pastime

Thirteen-year-old Max Kelmon lives in Palo Alto, California. Journalist Steve Henn describes Max's favorite pastime. "Behind the family kitchen in a converted garage, he has an Xbox, a big-screen TV, headphones and a microphone. There's an old couch covered in a sheet. And that couch where he parks himself . . . is one of Max's favorite places on the planet." Henn adds, "He spends hours, pretty much every day, honing his skill in Call of Duty."[1] Max's mother Vanessa talks about how important video games are to her son. "He could play Xbox for 12 straight hours," she says. "When I took it away, he started crying."[2]

While not all youth play video games for hours every day like Max, he is not unusual in his love of gaming; surveys show that most American youth do play video games at least some of the time. For example, in 2011 the market research company NPD Group reported that 91 percent of Americans ages two to seventeen play video games. Other studies show similar percentages. While in the past much of this youth game play occurred in teens, the NPD survey shows that the very young are quickly catching up. Its research shows that children between the ages of two and five composed the fastest-growing group of gamers between 2009 and 2011. Female players, another group that has traditionally lagged behind, are also catching up in recent years. Some of the youth who play video games only do so on occasion; however, many play every day like Max does. Much of this play occurs at home since the majority of youth have video game technology in their houses, including computers, game consoles, and smartphones. In a large 2010 study by the Kaiser Family Foundation, researchers found that 87 percent of youth ages eight to eighteen have a video game console in their home. Most game play occurs on consoles or computers; however, smartphones are increasing in popularity as game-playing devices. In addition to game time at home, many youth get even more game play at school because it is increasingly common for schools to incorporate video games as educational tools in the classroom.

Spending Hours Playing Games

All this game-play time adds up. Game designer and author Jane McGonigal estimates that by the time they are twenty-one, each young person, on average, will have spent about ten thousand hours gaming. She points out that this is a significant percentage of their lives. She says, "That's almost exactly as much time as they spend in a classroom during all of middle school and high school if they have perfect attendance."[3] Parents and researchers alike wonder about the effects of playing video games for this many hours. Critics fear that game play is detrimental to both mental and physical health. The American Academy of Child & Adolescent Psychiatry warns, "Children and adolescents can become overly involved and even obsessed with videogames. Spending large amounts of time playing these games can create problems."[4]

It warns that game play is associated with poor social skills, time away from family and other hobbies, lower grades in school, and decreased physical health. Critics are particularly concerned with the effects of playing violent games, arguing that these types of games increase the chances of aggressive and violent behavior and decrease empathy toward other people. However, video games also offer numerous potential benefits. They capture attention and engage youth like few other activities can. Researchers in a 2014 article in *American Psychologist* insist, "Game designers are wizards of engagement. They have mastered the art of pulling people of all ages into virtual environments, having them work toward meaningful goals, persevere in the face of multiple failures, and celebrate the rare moment of triumph after successfully completing challenging tasks."[5] Because games can make learning fun and engaging,

"Children and adolescents can become overly involved and even obsessed with videogames. Spending large amounts of time playing these games can create problems."[4]

—*The American Academy of Child & Adolescent Psychiatry, a nonprofit organization dedicated to improving the health of youth in the United States.*

Children between the ages of two and five make up the fastest-growing group of gamers in the last few years, surveys show. Many young people who play video games do so every day.

researchers believe they have the potential to be powerful tools for learning and social development.

Overall, the effect of video games on youth depends greatly on what the games are and how they are being played. Video game experts James Paul Gee and Elisabeth R. Hayes insist that it is impossible to simply categorize video games as either good or bad. Instead they maintain, "Their effects depend on how they are used and who is using them to what ends. It is a matter of context." They argue, "Video games . . . can be used for good or ill. They can be a productive use of time or a waste of time. It all depends on what we do with them."[6]

An Important Part of Youth Culture

No matter what the effects of video games are, it is clear that they are an important part of youth culture and will remain so in the future. In fact, youth video game play has been steadily increasing over time. The Entertainment Software Rating Board (ESRB)—the organization that assigns and enforces the video game rating system—reports explosive growth in the video game industry. In 2012 US computer and video game sales totaled $14.8 billion. This is more than double that of ten years earlier. The growing importance of video games to youth culture makes this an important topic to examine. Youth is a time of learning and development, and it is impossible for youth to spend large amounts of time playing video games and not be affected at all. With some young people spending as many hours playing games as they do in school, it is vital to consider the impact that these games have.

"Video games . . . can be used for good or ill. They can be a productive use of time or a waste of time. It all depends on what we do with them."[6]

—James Paul Gee and Elisabeth R. Hayes, researchers of video game effects and authors of Language and Learning in the Digital Age and Women and Gaming: The Sims and 21st Century Learning.

Video Games Research

Chapter One

Much of what researchers know about video games and youth comes from research studies. The research on games is extensive; psychologists and other experts have conducted hundreds of studies in an effort to understand how video game play affects young people. In addition, numerous studies of those studies have been made by researchers who reanalyze the data and come to their own conclusions. However, even with hundreds of studies to draw from, experts are deeply divided about how games affect youth.

Seeing Different Things

The problem is a lack of agreement about how to study the effect of video games. Most researchers agree that games likely influence youth to some extent, but the way a person thinks and behaves is affected by thousands of other factors too, and it is extremely difficult to understand the effect of games alone. This difficulty has led to continuing controversy in the field of games research. NPR journalist Shankar Vedantam explains that because of fundamental disagreements about how to study games, researchers simply cannot agree on many aspects of game research. He says, "The irony is that scientists who think the games are harmful and those who think they're not are both looking at the same evidence. They just see two different things."[7]

Vedantam illustrates this by comparing the findings of two leading games researchers, Brad Bushman and Christopher J. Ferguson. Both men have conducted extensive research on the effects of violent game play. Bushman talks about a study he directed in which participants played violent games, then researchers measured their aggression by allowing them to blast other people with loud, unpleasant noises. He says, "We try to make the noise as unpleasant as possible, by thinking of every noise you hate. So like, fingernails scratching on a chalkboard, dentist drills, sirens."[8] He says they could make the noise as loud as a smoke alarm, if they wanted to. Bushman found that the people who played violent games were more likely to act aggressively by blasting other people with loud noises. Based on this, he concludes that violent games make people more aggressive and less sensitive toward the feelings of others.

However, Ferguson has a different interpretation. He insists that studies such as Bushman's actually reveal little about aggression in the real world. In his opinion, the fact that research participants choose to blast others with loud noises does not mean they are more likely to engage in real aggression or violence outside the laboratory. He sees behavior changes such as those observed by Bushman as transient and trivial. He says, "We're talking about little children sticking their tongues out at each other and that sort of thing."[9] The differing opinions of Ferguson and Bushman help explain why there continues to be extensive controversy in the field of video games research. No matter how many studies are conducted, researchers continue to disagree about the design and interpretation of those studies.

Types of Research

Researchers investigate the effects of video games in a number of different ways. One common method is laboratory experimentation, such as Bushman's study where players could blast other people with loud noises. Laboratory experimentation involves recruiting participants and randomly assigning them to different groups. Researchers then apply different variables to the groups; for example, they might have one group play a solitary video game and the other play a game where they participate with others. They observe the behavior of the participants in order to reach conclusions about the effects of the variables they are testing. The benefit of laboratory research is that researchers have a high degree of control over the situation and the conditions that participants are exposed to. For example, they can have participants play a particular type of game for a defined period of time. This control means that researchers are better able to exclude other factors that may also influence the participant, and focus only on the effect of video games.

Researchers used versions of the Grand Theft Auto *video game to examine what effect violent games have on self-control. The study results suggest that violent video games reduce self-control in young players.*

In 2013 an example of a laboratory experiment involving video games was detailed in the journal *Social Psychology and Personality Science.* In that study, researchers randomly assigned a group of high school students to play either the nonviolent video game *Pinball 3D* or *Minigolf 3D* or the violent game *Grand Theft Auto III* or *Grand Theft Auto: San Andreas.* They placed a bowl of chocolate next to the computer and told gamers they could freely eat it. However, they warned them that eating a large amount of candy in a short period of time was unhealthy. Researchers then observed the participants. They found that those youth who played the violent games ate three times more chocolate than those who played the nonviolent games.

They interpreted this as evidence that violent games reduce youth self-control.

Researchers also study game effects through long-term studies in which they observe or interview participants on numerous different occasions over a longer period of time. A long-term study of video game effects was reported in the journal *Pediatrics* in 2011. Researchers studied a total of 3,034 youth in grades three, seven, and eight in order to explore the issue of video games and addiction. They surveyed the students three times—in 2007, 2008, and 2009—asking questions about their game play and behavior. They found that over that period of time, youth who reported that they were addicted to video games were also more likely to report that they were anxious, depressed, and performing poorly in school. One advantage of a long-term study such as this is that researchers can be more certain about results and trends because they make observations on multiple occasions.

Yet another way to research the effect of video games on youth is through correlational studies. In these studies researchers investigate whether a correlation exists between game playing and various other phenomena. For example, in 2012 the American Psychological Association (APA) published the results of a four-year correlational study involving more than five thousand US teenagers. The goal of the study was to investigate the correlation between playing M-rated games that glorify risk taking with reckless driving behavior. (Games rated M are intended for players seventeen and older.) Researchers examined the game-playing behavior of the teens and also their driving behavior and did find a correlation between the two. They found that teens who played video games with reckless driving behavior, such as *Grand Theft Auto III*, were more likely to have a number of different risky driving habits, including speeding and tailgating, and

"Playing violent video games causes an increase in the likelihood of physically aggressive behavior, aggressive thinking, aggressive affect, physiological arousal, and desensitization/low empathy."[13]

—Craig A. Anderson and Douglas A. Gentile, professors at Iowa State University who have conducted extensive research on video games, and Karen Dill-Shackleford (formerly Karen E. Dill), a social psychologist who studies media effects.

to be stopped by the police or involved in automobile accidents. An advantage of such a correlational study is that the behavior that researchers are observing is naturally occurring in the real world.

Problems with Games Research

The large body of existing research from all these types of studies provides a lot of information about how video game play affects youth; however, many of the studies also have limitations. A large percentage of gaming studies are conducted in a research laboratory so that researchers can have more control over what takes place. However, laboratory experiments can also be problematic because of this artificial setting. A lab setting controlled by researchers is not exactly the same as video game play in the real world. For instance, participants may play differently than they do at home or with friends. Or they may act differently when they know they are being observed. This means that it might not be valid to assume that if something happens in the laboratory it also happens in the real world; in other words, the results of a laboratory study may not apply to real life.

Another problem with the validity of the existing research is that much of it is focused on single-player games. This is because much game play was solitary in the past. However, technological developments in gaming now allow multiple players to take part in the same game—and research shows that a large number of them do so. It is likely that this social play influences youth in a different way. According to a 2013 report by the Entertainment Software Association (ESA)—the trade association of the US video game industry—62 percent of gamers take part in multiplayer games. With multiplayer games, participants constantly interact with other players, albeit in imaginary settings. With so many different people playing the same game at the same time, the experience differs each time a player logs on. Therefore, it is incorrect to assume that all players will be affected the same way by gaming, whether they play alone or with others. In a 2014 article in *American Psychologist*, researchers argue that "games that are fundamentally social and rely on varied social partners also provide a large amount of variability in game experiences, depending on who the player encounters each time she or he enters the gaming

Violent Game Play Causes Changes in the Brain

Researchers have observed that playing video games can cause changes in the player's brain. For example, in 2011 researchers from Indiana University School of Medicine in Indianapolis reported on a study in which they divided participants into two groups. One group played a first-person shooting game for a week, and the other group did not play violent games. Brain scans at the beginning and the end of the week showed that those young men who played violent games had less activity in the part of their brains that involved emotion, inhibition of impulses, and attention. In another study, conducted by Bruce Bartholow at the University of Missouri, participants played either a nonviolent video game or a violent one. After they played, researchers measured their brain response to a number of photos. They found that those people who had played violent games had a reduced brain response to photos of violence, such as a man holding a gun in another man's mouth.

world. Ultimately, these dynamic features mean that there is a certain amount of uniqueness to each player's experience, each time she or he plays even the very same game."[10] Such variability makes it extremely difficult to generalize about a game's effects because every player will experience the game in a different way.

A further difficulty with trying to understand the way video games affect youth is the existence of other variables that affect youth, in addition to game playing. The way young people think and act is also influenced by factors such as school, friends, exposure to other media such as music and movies, and family relationships. For example, a researcher might determine that a teenager who plays video games and also receives poor grades in school did poorly because of his game play. However, the poor grades could also be caused by many other factors such as family problems, bullying at school, or even a combination of different variables acting together. It is thus difficult for researchers to understand how video game play alone really influences youth.

Funding for Game Studies

Finally, the source of funding for a video game study can also influence the design and results of the study. For example, some game research has been funded by advocacy groups, which raises the possibility that the study results may be influenced by the interests of that group. For example, a group that wants government regulation of violent games might encourage a researcher to find that violent games harm youth, just as an industry group might encourage a researcher to come to the opposite conclusion. ESA representative Dan Hewitt insists that his organization has not been guilty of such influence. He says, "ESA hasn't funded any research in any way." According to Hewitt, "Everything that's out there and that we talk about is completely free from any ESA influence or financing."[11]

However, some research has been funded by organizations that may have an interest in certain types of results. For example, in 2011 British gaming writer John Walker investigated a study that found that game play has an effect on the brain. He reports that the study was funded by the Center for Successful Parenting. While Walker admits this does not necessarily influence the validity of the study, he points out that the organization is opposed to youth exposure to violent video games. This means it would benefit from research findings that show game violence is harmful.

> "Most earlier meta-analyses . . . considered a wide span of research from past decades. However this allows older research, potentially with less valid methods, to 'pollute' more recent and perhaps more valid research."[14]
>
> —Christopher J. Ferguson and John Kilburn, video games researchers and professors at Texas A&M International University.

Challenges in Studying Game Violence

A large percentage of the existing body of games research is about violent video games, and the validity of this type of research is particularly difficult to determine. This is because research about violent behavior often involves artificial measures and situations that are intended to represent violence. It would be unethical for researchers to allow participants to actually hurt other people or animals, so instead they must use abstract measures that stand for real-world violence.

Definitive answers are hard to come by in violent video game studies. Some researchers say they find clear links between violent games and aggressive behavior while others say the studies and findings are flawed.

For example, they use the noise blast, which gives participants have the ability to subject other people to an unpleasant sound. The length and volume that they choose is seen as a measure of their aggression. However, the noise blast illustrates the difficulty with using abstract measures to represent violence. The Media Coalition points out the difficulty of knowing whether a participant's choice of blast level can really be used to make conclusions about violence in the real world. It says, "What does the blast mean? Is a level of six 'aggressive' enough, or must it be eight or nine? Researchers—even the same researchers—using this measure have done so inconsistently in different studies. And is an irritating blast of "whishing" white noise similar to radio static . . . given to an unseen, un-reacting person a good surrogate for hurting an actual person? Maybe, maybe not."[12] Questions like these reveal the widespread disagreement over the validity of research on violent games.

Media Effects and the Advertising Industry

Ironically, while games researchers refuse to agree on whether video games have a lasting impact on youth, society generally accepts the reality of media effects in other realms. For example, the advertising industry thrives on the premise that media does have a significant effect on people of all ages. Advertising companies recognize that people can be greatly impacted by what they see in the media. As a result, advertising companies spend billions of dollars advertising various products through the media, many of them specifically targeted to youth. Another example of society's acceptance of the reality of media effects is that US television does not air sexually explicit shows during primetime hours when youth are likely to be watching. This is because it is widely agreed that exposure to sexually explicit media content can cause significant harm to young people.

Violent Video Games Research

Overall, strong support exists on both sides of the debate about video game violence, and definitive answers will not be found in the near future. On one side, researchers insist that numerous studies show a link between violent game play and negative behaviors including aggression. Game researchers Craig A. Anderson, Douglas A. Gentile, and Karen E. Dill conducted a major review of existing research in 2010 that shows this link. The researchers used the results from more than 130 research reports. Based on the data from all these studies they concluded that exposure to violent video games is unquestionably related to higher levels of aggressive behavior and to increased aggressive thinking. They state, "The main findings can be succinctly summarized: Playing violent video games causes an increase in the likelihood of physically aggressive behavior, aggressive thinking, aggressive affect, physiological arousal, and desensitization/low empathy. It also decreases helpful or prosocial behavior."[13] In addition, they state that their review shows these effects for both males and females and for numerous different cultures, including the United States, Japan, and Europe.

However, critics charge that many of these studies are meaningless because they have too many flaws. Ferguson conducted his own major review of existing studies, and unlike Anderson, Gentile and Dill, he did not find evidence that violent game play has a negative impact. Unlike Anderson, Gentile, and Dill's study, which included all research up until 2008, his was limited to research done from 1998 to 2008 and comprised a total of twenty-five studies. However, he insists that his analysis is the most useful because it includes only valid studies. He points out that many other analyses such as Bushman's and Anderson, Gentile, and Dill's include a large percentage of the existing research. However he believes that much of the old research is poorly constructed and may have invalid results. As a result, he argues, using all the research "allows older research, potentially with less valid methods, to 'pollute' more recent and perhaps more valid research."[14]

No Answers in Sight

Game violence is the most popular and controversial research topic for video game researchers. However, there is similar disagreement among researchers on many other aspects of game play; for example, whether it is beneficial or harmful to mental health and whether video games should be used to help teach youth in school. As a result of such disagreement, society continues to struggle to understand how video games really affect youth, and researchers continue to study this topic.

In January 2013 US president Barack Obama urged even more research to help society understand video games, specifically those games with violent content. He asked Congress to support a bill that would give the Centers for Disease Control and Prevention (CDC) $10 million to study the effects of violent media, including video games. He said, "Congress should fund research into the effects that violent video games have on young minds. We don't benefit from ignorance. We don't benefit from not knowing the

"Congress should fund research into the effects that violent video games have on young minds. We don't benefit from ignorance. We don't benefit from not knowing the science."[15]

—Barack Obama, forty-fourth president of the United States.

science."[15] While it is true that society would benefit from answers about the effects of video games, the fact is that hundreds of studies on video games already exist, and there is strong support for opinions on both sides of gaming debates. It thus appears unlikely that even such a substantial research effort will provide any definitive answers about video games.

Violent Game Play

Chapter Two

On April 20, 1999, Colorado teenagers Dylan Klebold and Eric Harris walked into Columbine High School and placed two home-made bombs in the cafeteria. They then waited at the school's exits, intending to shoot students who tried to escape after the bombs exploded. The bombs failed to explode, however, so the teens reentered the school with guns hidden underneath their trench coats and went on a shooting rampage. They killed thirteen people and injured more than twenty, some of whom were left paralyzed. The boys appeared to enjoy what they were doing. Survivors even remember hearing one of them say, "Maybe we should start knifing people. That might be more fun."[16] Finally, Klebold and Harris killed themselves, ending the deadliest high school shooting in US history.

Many people believe that violent video game play contributed to this massacre and that playing violent games has a negative impact on youth in general. Both Klebold and Harris reportedly spent large amounts of time playing the video game *Doom*, in which players use shotguns and rocket launchers to kill zombies and demons. Two years after the shooting some of the victims' parents even sued a number of software companies, including the one that created *Doom*, arguing that these violent games contributed to the murders. Yet others contend that there is absolutely no evidence that violent games are harmful. In fact, some researchers argue that violent game play can actually benefit youth in many ways. This topic continues to provoke intense debate, particularly following events like that which occurred at Columbine.

Many Youth Play Violent Games

Research reveals that many youth do play video games like *Doom* with violent content. For example, in 2012 the APA published the results of a four-year study involving more than five thousand US teenagers. Fifty percent of the teens reported in an interview that their parents allowed them to play games rated M, meaning that they are intended for those seventeen and older. M-rated games frequently receive that rating because they contain high levels of violence. Of the youth who had played M-rated games in the study, 12 percent had played *Manhunt*, and 58 percent had played *Grand Theft Auto III*. Both of these games are extremely violent. In a 2011 Supreme Court decision about video game violence, Justice Samuel Alito describes the content of violent games such as *Manhunt* and *Grand Theft Auto*. He says: "In some of these games, the violence is astounding. Victims by the dozens are killed with every imaginable implement, including machine guns, shotguns, clubs, hammers, axes, swords, and chainsaws. Victims are dismembered, decapitated, disemboweled, set on fire, and chopped into little pieces. They cry out in agony and beg for mercy. Blood gushes, splatters, and pools. Severed body parts and gobs of human remains are graphically shown."[17]

> "In some of these games, the violence is astounding. Victims by the dozens are killed with every imaginable implement."[17]
>
> —Samuel Alito, justice of the US Supreme Court.

Increased Realism

Not only is violent game play common for youth, but violent games are becoming more and more realistic. Increasingly sophisticated technology and storylines mean that in many games the player feels like he or she is part of the game, engaging in the same violent acts as his or her on-screen character is doing. One example of a game that so engages players is *DayZ*. In this multiplayer zombie apocalypse game players have only one life and lose everything if they are killed. They spend the game looking for survival resources and trying to avoid being killed by zombies or other players. One player relates his story of being caught by surprise and accidentally killing another *DayZ* player. He says this had a huge emotional impact on him. He describes the encounter: "I was running out of the woods in the middle of nowhere and a fully loaded player runs RIGHT in front of me and keeps going. They couldn't of been more than 10 feet away. . . . I turned around and unloaded an entire M4 20 round clip into his back. He died instantly." The player says he felt guilty and upset by what had happened.

> As soon as I realized what I had done, I felt horrible. This wave of grief ran over my body. All I could think about was the hours and hours this player must have spent scouring apartments, barns, and military bases [for survival supplies]. . . . This player had everything a person could want. Every attachment for his guns. Hundreds of rounds of ammo. I took it away from him in a second and he didn't even see me coming. We were not in a firefight and he wasn't threatening me. I just shot him in the back.[18]

Columbine High School students exit their classrooms during a 1999 shooting spree that killed thirteen people. The two young shooters were reported to have spent large amounts of time playing the violent video game Doom.

Crime Rates and Video Games

One way to investigate the relationship between violent video games and violent behavior is to examine crime rates. If game violence causes real-world violence, increases in video game play should be accompanied by increases in violent crime. However, researchers have found that the opposite is true. Since the 1990s video game playing has dramatically increased in many countries, including the United States, Britain, and Japan. A significant number of the games being played are violent. However, over this same period of time violent crime rates have dropped in these nations. According to the CDC, between 1995 and 2011 the violent crime arrest rate for males ages ten to twenty-four dropped from about 850 arrests per 100,000 to only about 423. The Media Coalition points out that, overall, the majority of youth play games without committing seriously violent acts. It says, "Just about all American kids play video games. . . . Meanwhile, less than one-fourth of 1 percent of the U.S. juvenile population was arrested for serious crimes in 2010. Spectacular crimes like school shootings are even rarer."

Media Coalition, "Only a Game: Why Censoring New Media Won't Stop Gun Violence," 2013. www.mediacoalition.org.

Changing the Way Youth Understand Violence

Critics argue that continual exposure to violence causes harmful desensitization in youth. This means that as they are continually exposed to violence in video games, youth become so accustomed to it that when they experience violence in real life they are less likely to be upset or even affected by it. Brad Bushman found this result in a study during which he showed students pictures of a man shoving a gun down another man's throat and of a man holding a knife to a woman's throat. He says, "What we found is for people who were exposed to a lot of violent video games, their brains did not respond to the violent images."[19] Instead they were numb. As a result of being desensitized to violence, youth may be less sensitive to the pain and suffering of other people.

Exposure to game violence can also make violence seem like a normal and acceptable way to behave. Researchers Craig A. Anderson and Wayne W. Warburton talk about how the brain learns things through repeated exposure. They say: "The brain is a neural network in which concepts, ideas, feelings, and memories are stored and interconnected. The way this network 'wires up' depends on what people experience."[20] In the case of violent games, researchers like Anderson and Warburton believe that when youth repeatedly play these games, their brains become wired to see violence as normal behavior.

Young people who are exposed to a great deal of game violence can also come to view violence as having no harmful consequences. In the real world, an individual who engages in violence against others is subject to punishment. For example, shooting another person might result in a jail sentence. However, in video games shooting another person usually goes unpunished. Journalist Scott Shackford gives the example of the extremely popular game *Grand Theft Auto V*. He says, "Grand Theft Auto V is a violent, profane sandbox, allowing players the freedom to engage in the sorts of brutal behavior for which we tend to lock people up for long periods of time (sometimes ending with a trip to an execution chamber)."[21]

A 1997 shooting by sixteen-year-old Evan Ramsey illustrates the way that violent game play like in *Grand Theft Auto* can distort youths' understanding of violent behavior. Ramsey took a shotgun into his high school in Bethel, Alaska, and killed the school principal and a student. In a later interview, however, he admitted that playing video games left him unable to properly understand the severity of what he was doing. He says that he did not understand that unlike in a video game, shooting somebody had permanent and serious consequences. "I honestly believed that if you shoot somebody, that they would get back up." Ramsey also states, "I didn't realize that you shoot somebody, they die."[22]

> "What we found [in our research] is for people who were exposed to a lot of violent video game, their brains did not respond to the violent images."[19]
>
> —Brad Bushman, who has conducted extensive research on the effects of violent games.

An Effective Way to Teach Violence

In addition to influencing the way people think about violence, violent games can actively teach youth to be violent. Overall, there is strong evidence that video games are an excellent teaching tool. For example, the military regularly uses games like flight simulators for training. Just as flight simulators are extremely effective at teaching pilots how to fly, violent games are powerful forces that teach players to be violent. One thing that makes video games such an effective teaching tool is that players actively participate. Anderson and Warburton explain why this matters. They say, "Active participation assists learning as it requires attention, and closely attending to a task assists people to memorize the relevant behaviors and knowledge."[23] Another way researchers believe violent games encourage violent behavior is that they reward players for being violent. Bushman explains, "You get points when you kill people. If you kill enough people, you get to advance to the next level of the game."

Some experts warn that extensive exposure to video game violence can lead young people to view violence as having no harmful consequences. They might even begin to see violence as normal behavior.

In addition, he says, "You are also rewarded through things that you might hear. If you kill somebody, maybe you hear, 'Impressive, nice shot, you are tied for the lead.'"[24] The result of such rewards and praise is that it increases the likelihood that players will repeat that behavior.

In 2011 Norwegian Anders Behring Breivik shot sixty-nine people dead and wounded hundreds of others on Utoya Island in Norway. In his manifesto he reveals that he played the video game *Call of Duty: Modern Warfare 2* as part of his training for the shooting. He says, "I just bought Modern Warfare 2, the game. It is probably the best military simulator out there." Breivik says the game was a very realistic and effective way to train for the shooting. He says, "I've still learned to love it . . . and especially the multiplayer part is amazing. You can more or less completely simulate actual operations."[25]

> "I honestly believed that if you shoot somebody, that they would get back up [like in a video game]."[22]
>
> —Evan Ramsey, who shot and killed two people in an Alaska high school in 1997.

A Way to Release Aggression

While researchers such as Anderson, Warburton, and Bushman believe that violent games cause youth to go out and commit violent acts in the real world, other researchers believe that the effect is actually the opposite. They insist that violent game play actually prevents youth from engaging in violence because it keeps them busy and allows them to release their aggression through game play, in which no real people are harmed. Robert VerBruggen, deputy managing editor of *National Review*, argues, "Taking away video-game violence would actually increase real violence, because these people [with violent tendencies] would lose an outlet." He believes that rather than inspiring violent behavior, violent video games keep violent people busy. He says, "Every minute they spend with a controller in their hands is a minute they don't spend hurting others."[26]

Video game player Aaron Sampson says that he plays violent games to help him release stress in a harmless way. He believes that the ability to release his frustration in this way prevents him from

27

doing anything harmful or violent in real life. For example, he says that in college he got into a confrontation with a teacher, but thanks in part to the fact that he used violent game play as an outlet for his anger, he was able to control himself and drop out of the class rather than let the confrontation escalate. He compares his behavior with another student who was not able to release stress harmlessly. That angry student shot and killed a teacher the following year. Sampson says, "That event has always made me stop and think: What is the difference between a guy like me, who was angry and had access to firearms, but used some unkind words and non-violent actions, versus someone who decides to shoot up a school?" Sampson believes his violent game play was one important factor. He argues, "When I hear Senators talking about violent video games and the media making false correlations between violent video games, firearms, and actual violence, I want to stop these people from making a huge mistake and eliminating one of the most calming factors of my life."[27]

An Important Part of Development

In addition to helping youth defuse anger and frustration, there is evidence that exposure to violence in games is actually an important part of development. The fact is that all youth will be exposed to violence throughout their lives because that is part of the world. By experiencing it in the safe environment of a video game, they can learn to manage their fear and deal with violence. Writer Michael Venables insists that for this reason parents should not be so quick to keep their children away from violent games. He says, "As twenty-first century parents, we tend to protect our children from 'issues' like fear and violence. But, when exposed to scary content, children can learn to cope with and overcome fear." In his opinion, "Perhaps it's time to allow them to teach themselves with different fantasy worlds."[28]

Some people worry that video games can have such a powerful effect over youth that they may be unable to distinguish between the fantasy game world and the real world. However, gamers insist this is not true. James Paul Gee and Elisabeth R. Hayes argue that even young people possess the critical thinking skills that allow them to easily distinguish between fantasy and reality. They say, "All mentally

Some gamers, and some experts, say that violent video games provide a harmless outlet for relieving stress and aggression. For some young people these games might even provide a way to manage fears of real-world violence.

healthy people—as well as some mentally unhealthy people—know the difference between screens (and fiction generally) and reality." They insist that if a person cannot make this distinction, then the types of games being played is the least of his or her problems. They state, "People who do not know the difference are missing critical

Reenacting Video Games

In some cases teenagers who have killed others in violent acts appear to have been reenacting specific violent video games, suggesting that these games can inspire real-world violence. For example, in 2003 eighteen-year-old Devin Moore was taken to an Alabama police station after officers found him sleeping in a stolen car. Inside the police station he took a gun from one of the officers and opened fire, killing three people. He then stole a police car in order to escape. After his arrest he reportedly said, "Life is like a video game. Everybody's got to die sometime." Willie Crump, whose son was one of those killed, points out, "Everything he did is right from Grand Theft Auto." He asks, "Why would you make a game like that to show kids how to kill cops?" In another case, in 2007 Colorado teens Heather Trujillo and her boyfriend Lamar Roberts killed her seven-year-old sister Zoe after practicing a variety of *Mortal Kombat* moves on her, including hitting her, kicking her, and even dropping her. Zoe died with a broken wrist, more than twenty bruises, bleeding in her neck muscles and under her spine, and swelling in her brain.

Quoted in Alex Tresniowski, "Driven to Kill," *People*, September 26, 2005. www.people.com.

faculties and are dangerous to themselves and others in all sorts of ways, well beyond what video games they play."[29]

Media expert Cheryl K. Olson argues that the nature of video games is that they are intended to be pretend and not related to the way people can or should act in the real world. She insists that most players implicitly know this. For example, she talks about the game *Postal*. According to Olson, "A trailer for Postal 3 . . . encourages players to 'Tase those annoying hockey moms or shoot them in the face!'" Olson says that while this might sound disturbing, it is actually meant to be ridiculous. "The game is deliberately outrageous," she says, and adds, "Young people know it: as one 13-year-old said during a study I conducted at Harvard, 'With video games, you know it's fake.'"[30] Olson believes that fears about the way such game violence might harm youth are missing the point that many of these games are clearly make-believe and understood as such.

Mass Shootings

Shootings such as the Columbine massacre have intensified the controversy over video game violence, with some people asking whether violent games might be a cause of these shootings. Proponents of this theory point to the fact that many shooters have also played violent video games and theorize that their gameplay inspired them to shoot people in real life. However, critics point out that hundreds of other factors could have also played a role, such as whether the youth were bullied or whether they had a good family relationship. In addition, the fact is that millions of youth play violent games, and mass shootings are relatively rare. *Forbes* writer Paul Tassi says, "99.99999% of gamers who play even the most gruesome of titles do not end up killing anyone."[31] Overall, most experts believe that while violent games are not solely to blame for mass shootings, they can be a risk factor. Former FBI profiler Mary Ellen O'Toole explains, "We see them as sources of fueling ideation that's already there."[32]

"We see . . . [video games] as sources of fueling ideation that's already there."[32]

—Mary Ellen O'Toole, a former profiler for the Federal Bureau of Investigation.

No matter what their effect, violent games remain popular among youth. According to the ESA, in 2012 the top-selling video game was the violent M-rated *Call of Duty: Black Ops II*. Of the top ten games that year, a total of five were violent with M ratings. A sixth contained cartoon violence. It is likely that many of these games are being played by youth. What is less certain is how these youth are being affected.

Video Games and Health

When he was fourteen years old Californian Nick Hayes developed Ewing's sarcoma, a bone cancer. His treatment included multiple surgeries and sessions of chemotherapy, but it also included video game play. Hayes played *Re-Mission*, a video game specifically designed to help young cancer patients understand their illness and manage their treatment regimens. According to doctors, it is very challenging for young people to properly understand and adhere to cancer treatments because they cannot actually see what is happening inside their bodies. This makes it difficult for them to really understand the necessity of difficult treatments that may make them feel unwell. *Re-Mission*, and its sequel, *Re-Mission 2*, increase understanding because they are set inside the human body. As they play the games youth can see what happens in the body during treatment. These games also help players feel empowered in their treatment because game play actively involves them in the process of destroying cancer with various weapons such as chemotherapy and cells in the body's immune system. Hayes says that playing *Re-Mission* made him feel like he was doing something to help. He says, "I loved it." He explains, "I remember in certain stages of the game you were fighting leukemia and bone cancers, and these were things I had. I felt like I was able to fight them as well."[33] A 2008 study of *Re-Mission* found that Hayes's experience is common; researchers found that overall, youth who played the game had a greatly improved understanding of their treatment and adherence to their treatment regimen.

A Tool to Improve Health

As this example shows, video game play has the potential to be far more than simple entertainment. It can have a significant impact on young people's physical and mental health. In the case of the *Re-Mission* games, that impact is highly beneficial; *Re-Mission* players tend to have improved mental health because they better understand their illness, and their chances of surviving the cancer are increased because they are more likely to follow their treatment regimens.

Another example of using games to benefit health is occurring in New Zealand. Researchers there have created the game *SPARX*, to help youth who suffer from depression. In this game players adopt a warrior avatar and move through different levels of a fantasy world. At the same time though, the game is teaching them to understand and cope with their depression. *Time* journalist Maia Szalavitz explains the game: "The players move through seven levels of a fantasy world, starting in the Cave Province, which teaches basic information about depression and offers hope for recovery. Next comes the Ice Province, which promotes activity and teaches relaxation techniques. The Volcano Province provides lessons on coping with intense emotions like anger, while the subsequent Mountain, Swamp and Bridgeland regions focus on addressing specific problems and recognizing and diffusing unhelpful thoughts."[34] Researchers studied the effectiveness of *SPARX* on 168 teens who had sought help for depression. Approximately 44 percent of those who played the game recovered completely from depression, compared with only 26 percent of those who underwent regular treatment.

> "I remember in certain stages of the game you were fighting leukemia and bone cancers, and these were things I had. I felt like I was able to fight them as well."[33]
>
> —Nick Hayes, who suffered from bone cancer when he was fourteen years old.

Even for youth who are not suffering from serious illnesses such as depression, there is evidence that video game play can enhance mental health. Numerous studies show that playing video games can leave young people feeling more positive, confident, and better able to deal with the ups and downs of everyday life. In 2013 researchers from the Gaming Research Group and Young and Well Cooperative Research Centre in Australia published the results of a comprehensive review of more than two hundred research studies and papers from around the world. Their goal was to investigate the impact of video game play on young people's mental health, and their conclusions were overwhelmingly positive. They report: "We found that playing video

A teacher works with a girl who has undergone a bone marrow transplant for cancer. Video games are being used for many purposes, including helping young cancer patients understand their illness and treatments.

games positively influences young people's emotional state, vitality, engagement, competence and self-acceptance. And that it's associated with higher self-esteem, optimism, resilience, healthy relationships and social connections and functioning."[35]

Addiction

However, the effects of video game play on mental health are not universally positive. Some youth become pathologically addicted to playing video games, meaning that they become so preoccupied with gaming that they ignore other important parts of their life such as school and relationships with friends and family. There is no doubt that such addiction can have many negative effects. Researcher Douglas Gentile was part of a study on video game addiction involving youth in Singapore. He reports that this study and others show that addiction is a problem for a significant percentage of youth. Gentile says, "We're starting to see a number of studies from different cultures—in

34

Europe, the U.S. and Asia—and they're all showing that somewhere around 7 to 11 percent of gamers seem to be having real problems to the point that they're considered pathological gamers."[36] His two-year study of 3,034 third through eighth grade students in Singapore showed that addiction results in serious problems for youth, including anxiety, depression, social phobias, and lower school performance.

Liz Woolley, founder of the website On-Line Gamers Anonymous, has personal experience with video game addiction. She says, "I want to warn people that these games can take control of their lives just like drugs or alcohol."[37] According to Woolley, her son Shawn became addicted to the online game *Everquest*, and it was all he could think about. For instance, she says, at his brother's wedding he disappeared during the ceremony and did not come back. "People noticed that he wasn't at the reception and I discovered he had left in the middle of the wedding and walked home to continue playing his game." She says, "My son would have never done that before his addiction. He loved parties and socializing."[38] Woolley's son later committed suicide, and she believes it was the result of his game addiction.

Just as people suffering from addiction to drugs and alcohol go to rehabilitation centers, some video game addicts also go to rehab to get over their addictions. The reSTART center outside Seattle is one center that helps video-game and other technology addicts recover. Founder Hilarie Cash explains that addiction is a serious problem for many people. She says that for people who are addicted, their condition controls the way they behave and can interfere with exercise, sleep, and time with friends and family. For many youth gaming addiction can strike when they go away to college, she says, because parents are no longer able to moderate their gaming activity. Isaac Vaisburg experienced this and had to go through the reSTART program twice before he recovered. Vaisburg says he dropped out of the program the first time and went back to college, but his life immediately became consumed by game play again. One Saturday, he

"Somewhere around 7 to 11 percent of gamers seem to be having real problems to the point that they're considered pathological gamers."[36]

—Douglas Gentile, a researcher who has conducted numerous studies of video game effects.

says, he downloaded a game and did not stop playing it for forty-two hours. "And then I slept," he says, "I slept through my first class Monday, and I didn't go to class the rest of that day, and the day after, or for five weeks after that."[39]

Video game addiction is not officially recognized as a disorder in the United States; however, in 2013 the American Psychiatric Association (APA) took a step toward recognizing it as one. In that year it released an updated version of the *Diagnostic and Statistical Manual of Mental Disorders*, the manual that researchers and clinicians use to diagnose and classify mental disorders. In this update the APA mentions something called "internet use gaming disorder," which includes video game play. The APA describes this condition. It says, "The 'gamers' play compulsively, to the exclusion of other interests, and their persistent and recurrent online activity results in clinically significant impairment or distress. People with this condition endanger their academic or job functioning because of the amount of time they spend playing. They experience symptoms of withdrawal when pulled away from gaming."[40] Internet gaming disorder is not formally classified as a disorder in the 2013 update; however, it is included as a condition warranting more research to determine whether it should be classified as a disorder in the future.

> "I want to warn people that these games can take control of their lives just like drugs or alcohol."[37]
>
> —Liz Woolley, founder of the website On-Line Gamers Anonymous.

Gaming and Social Relationships

Even for youth who are not pathologically addicted, video games can have a negative impact on mental health if they are played in a way that causes social isolation. In some cases youth spend large quantities of time playing games alone. As a result, they rarely interact with real people. This lack of interaction can be harmful to social development and overall mental health. The website Video Game Addiction warns that isolation can cause lasting harm. It says that if a teen does not socialize with peers, "[he] won't develop effective social skills, which will hinder his ability to develop and maintain healthy relationships in college and beyond. Suddenly,

World of Warcraft Enhances Social Relationships

World of Warcraft (*WoW*) is a popular video game that some people play for hours a day. It is a massive multiplayer online game in which players from all over the world interact in a virtual world. The game allows them to form groups, complete quests, meet friends, and compete in tournaments. *WoW* challenges the stereotype of gaming as causing harmful isolation because players typically engage in extensive social interaction with others. One *WoW* gamer says, "My fiance and I have been on WOW since shortly after it went live, and we have a wonderful social guild [a group that players can join]. . . . Through out the course of playing we have met some really wonderful people and call them friends." He says that they have even met some of these people in person, once inviting two of them to stay at their house when they were traveling in the area. Overall, he believes *WoW* is an important part of his social network. He says, "We never would have met these great friends without WOW!! Our guild is an extended family for us."

Gill, comment to Elizabeth Harper, "What Have You Done Because of *WoW?*," blog, *Wow Insider*, February 14, 2014. http://wow.joystiq.com.

he's 21 but has the social skills of a 15-year-old. He doesn't know how to make friends, talk to girls, or just 'hang out' and enjoy people's company."[41]

However, while some youth do play video games in isolation, the majority actually report that game play is a very social activity. Playing a video game does not necessarily mean playing alone. Instead, technology gives youth the ability to play games directly with friends; for example, Wii games like *Just Dance* or *Super Mario*. Youth can also play with a group of people online in a game like *Everquest*, a fantasy game where players create a character such as a human, an elf, or even a cat-person and interact with other players as they explore a fantasy world. Cheryl K. Olson has studied the game play of a large number of youth. She says that while people often view video

Food-Related Games May Make Youth Eat More

Some video games are centered on food; for example, players might run a pizza restaurant or a candy factory. However, a new study suggests that these types of games may lead to unhealthy eating. In 2013 Dutch researchers revealed the results of a study of eight- to ten-year-olds, which show that children who play food-themed games might be more likely to eat more food and more junk food. In the study some participants played a game that involved a fruit or a popular brand of candy. Others played a game that did not involve food. After they played, the youth were offered bowls with apples, sliced bananas, jelly candy, and chocolate. Researchers found that everyone who played a food-themed game—even the fruit one—ate more food and more candy.

gaming as an isolating activity—for example a youth playing alone in the basement—her research does not support this belief. Instead, she says, "The children we studied saw video games as intensely social."[42] According to Olson, video games actually facilitate social interaction by providing a focus for conversation and a structure around which youth hang out with one another. Data from the ESA also shows evidence that much game play is social. It reports that 62 percent of gamers play video games with other people, either in person or online.

Jane McGonigal, director of game research and development at the Institute for the Future, believes that video games are actually a solution to the problem of social isolation. Research shows that members of society have become increasingly disconnected from one another in recent years due to factors such as busy lives and long commutes that leave them less time and energy for socializing with others. McGonigal argues that gaming is actually helping to reverse that problem. She explains that a large number of games involve interaction with others and that people can easily engage in this interaction from wherever they are, rather than having to travel to meet friends.

For example, she says, millions of people participate in games like *FarmVille* on social networks, where they help others or send them gifts, or they belong to online game worlds like *World of Warcraft*, where they interact with other people in that world. Overall, McGonigal insists that games are one of the few things connecting members of society in an otherwise increasingly disconnected world. She says, "Games are increasingly a crucial social thread woven throughout our everyday lives."[43]

Games and Physical Health

In addition to affecting mental health, video game play can impact physical health. In some cases it is detrimental because it results in less exercise. Most game play involves sitting in front of a screen for long periods of time, and youth who do this have less time to spend on being physically active. Exercise is an important part of staying physically and mentally healthy. However, it is widely agreed that youth in the United States do not spend enough time engaged in physical activity. Many people believe this is part of the reason for the increasing rate of childhood obesity and related health problems. Childhood obesity has become a serious problem. According to the CDC, in the past thirty years it has more than doubled in children and tripled in adolescents. It is estimated that one-third of youth are obese, and as a result of being overweight these youth are at higher risk for numerous health problems including high blood pressure and type 2 diabetes as well as psychological problems such as negative body image and depression. The American Heart Association says, "Childhood obesity is now the No. 1 health concern among parents in the United States."[44] As a result of the obesity problem, experts are urging youth to be more active.

One type of video game—called exergames—offers a possible solution to that problem. In exergaming players must physically move to play the game; for example, dance or pretend to hit a ball. They hold a controller that responds to their movements. Game player

> "Games are increasingly a crucial social thread woven throughout our everyday lives."[43]
>
> —Jane McGonigal, game designer and author of *Reality Is Broken: Why Games Make Us Better and How They Can Change the World.*

Two young people test their tennis skills and have fun with a Nintendo Wii video game. Some studies suggest such games are a good form of exercise while others question whether they have any physical fitness benefits.

Matthew Cod describes one of these games, *Just Dance 4*. He says, "If you've never played any of the Just Dance series before, the concept is very straightforward—you dance, mimicking the steps of on screen dancers, and earn points based on your accuracy. Where other rhythm games have you pressing buttons, tapping a touchscreen, or stepping on dance mat in time to the beat, Just Dance goes a step further by using your Wii Remote (or Kinect or PlayStation Move on the other consoles) to track your movements." The result is that a significant amount of physical activity is required in order to play the game well. Cod says he quickly worked up a sweat with this game and warns, "Just Dance 2014 should probably come packaged with a hand towel."[45]

Exergaming and Fitness

There is some evidence that exergames are just as effective as traditional forms of exercise in keeping youth physically fit. In a study published in 2011 in the *Archives of Pediatrics and Adolescent Medicine* researchers Bruce Bailey and Kyle McInnis tested 39 boys and girls between 9 and 13 years old as they played six different exergames, including a dance game and a boxing game. The researchers measured how much energy they were expending with a machine that tested their breathing. They found that for most of the games, the participants expended at least as much energy as they would when engaged in a moderate form of exercise such as walking. In another study, researchers found that playing exergames with others can help overweight teens lose weight. In a study published in *Obesity* in 2013, researchers studied 54 overweight and obese adolescents, ages 15 to 19. Participants were encouraged to play the Nintendo Wii *Active* game for 30 to 60 minutes per school day. After 20 weeks, those who played the game cooperatively with a friend had lost weight.

However, despite such optimism about the future of exergaming, there are also a number of studies showing no connection between exergaming and increased physical activity. For example, in February 2012 the journal *Pediatrics* published a study on exergaming in which eighty-four children received Wii consoles. Half of the children were given exercise games like *Wii Sports*, and the other half received games that can be played from a seated position. The researchers did not find evidence that having an exergame increased physical activity. They report, "There was no evidence that children receiving the active video games were more active in general, or at any time, than children receiving the inactive video games."[46] Other studies also show a similar lack of support for video games as a fitness tool.

"You are what you eat" is a popular saying that reminds people that the food they consume has a significant impact on the way their bodies function. Craig A. Anderson and Wayne A. Warburton suggest that society might think of video games in the same way, recognizing that the games people consume have an influence on their minds and bodies. They recommend that youth think about what that influence is and make choices accordingly. They state, "As with food, there are media that are good to consume regularly (in moderation), media that are for infrequent consumption and media that children should avoid."[47]

Games and Learning

In the 2011–2012 school year Peter Tromba, the principal of Monroe Middle School in Eugene, Oregon, created a pilot class centered on the popular video game *Minecraft*. In *Minecraft* players create and break apart various kinds of blocks in three-dimensional worlds. The students in Tromba's class started building a simple pyramid. Next they researched and constructed medieval castles. By the end of the class they had become skilled enough in *Minecraft* to replicate the floor plan of their middle school. Tromba believes that playing the game helped his students develop many important skills, including innovation, problem solving, and decision making. He argues that while *Minecraft* is a video game, it is also a very effective tool for understanding concepts such as architecture in the real world. He explains, "They . . . experienced the physical layouts from a first-person perspective and were much more fluent in the architectural topics as they constructed and explored." Overall, he argues, "it was clear that the physics of a game engine or other artificial reality can inform students' understanding of the real world."[48] Also important was that *Minecraft* made learning fun. According to Tromba, attendance improved for every student in the class, and both students and parents were enthusiastic about the knowledge and skills being gained from the game.

A Powerful Tool for Learning

Tromba is not the only one to recognize the potential of video games as a teaching tool. Learning is at the core of almost every video game. In fact, in order to play successfully gamers must learn to strategize and solve problems. James Paul Gee points out, "If they don't, they don't leave the first level of a game." For example, he talks about the popular game *Grand Theft Auto*. While many people might describe this game as an opportunity for players to go on a wild spree of criminal behavior, he points out that it is actually about learning. He says, "*Grand Theft Auto* is not about crime—it is about players coming up with good strategies for success in a world with multiple constraints."[49]

The video game *Foldit* illustrates the amazing potential of games to teach people extremely complex topics. In this game players learn about the shapes of proteins and compete online to fold them into the most efficient shapes possible. Researchers believe that some of the solutions coming from *Foldit* have the potential to help scientists develop cures for diseases like cancer and Alzheimer's disease. However, many of the people providing these complex solutions are not researchers who have spent years studying biology or chemistry. They are simply everyday people who have learned these skills through playing the game. Zoran Popovich, one of the creators of *Foldit*, says, "It has basically shown that it is possible to create experts in a particular domain purely through game play."[50] For example, Dallas massage therapist Scott Zaccanelli is one of the game's top players. Zaccanelli is not a scientist, yet *USA Today* reports that he was part of a team that figured out the structure of a protein that scientists had puzzled over for years. The report says, "In one of the game's most recent challenges, players analyzed a monkey HIV protein whose structure had eluded scientists for 15 years. Zaccanelli's team of *Foldit* players figured it out in 10 days."[51]

> "It was clear that the physics of a game engine or other artificial reality can inform students' understanding of the real world."[48]
>
> —Peter Tromba, principal of Monroe Middle School in Eugene, Oregon.

Cognitive Skills

Research shows that video games improve a number of different types of skills. Cognitive skills are one type that is enhanced by game play. Researchers have found that video game players often perform better than non–game players when their attention, accuracy, speed, multitasking, and vision are tested. Studies also show that these cognitive improvements appear to last for an extended period of time and to transfer to tasks other than video game play. In a 2014 article published

Shooter games may improve players' cognitive skills. These skills include attention, accuracy, speed, vision, and ability to multitask.

by the American Psychological Association (APA), researchers review numerous studies on game playing and find that shooter games are particularly effective at improving cognitive skills. The researchers state, "The most convincing evidence [on cognitive improvement] comes from the numerous training studies that recruit naive gamers (those who have hardly or never played *shooter* video games) and randomly assign them to play either a shooter video game or another type of video game for the same period of time."[52] According to the researchers, those participants who play the shooter games have much greater cognitive improvement than the participants who play other types of games.

Social Skills

Video games can also teach social skills. Researchers from the 2014 APA study point out that a large number of games involve interaction with other people in virtual communities. They argue that through these interactions players learn many social skills. They explain, "In these virtual social communities, decisions need to be made on the fly about whom to trust, whom to reject, and how to most effectively lead a group."[53] These skills can also be used in social interactions outside the game.

For youth who have trouble interacting with peers, video game play can be particularly beneficial. In real life it can be extremely challenging for young people who are shy or socially inept to interact with others. However, because video game worlds are make-believe and often anonymous, they can be less intimidating. Gaming helps youth practice social skills and gain confidence that can then be used in real-world interactions. One group of youth that often has trouble interacting with other people is those with autism. However, there is evidence that video game play can help autistic youth learn to communicate more effectively. One mother says of her autistic son, "He struggled to make friends. He found (and finds) expressions difficult to read, hints impossible to pick up and so on. His concept (or lack) of personal space made him irritating to his school mates." She says video games have helped change this. She says that her son played *Minecraft* with his friend over Xbox Live, which allows the players to talk while playing together. According to her, "[It] helped no end. He was able to talk to them in a way that much suited his social communication style, he was able to showcase his awesome Minecraft skills (his Autistic traits lend themselves very well here), which helped boost his street cred. And then because he'd made these connections on his terms outside of school, those friendships started to blossom in school too."[54]

> "The video game [*Foldit*] has basically shown that it is possible to create experts in a particular domain purely through game play."[50]
>
> —Zoran Popovich, one of the creators of Foldit, a game in which players learn about the shapes of proteins and compete online to fold them into the most efficient shapes possible.

Understanding the Human Experience

In addition to improving social skills, some evidence suggests that video games can help youth develop a better understanding of what it means to be human and to develop empathy for other people. *Forbes* contributor Erik Kain points out that young people learn important lessons about life by studying the experiences of other people who are different from them. Reading is one way this happens, and this is one of the reasons that youth read and analyze various books in school. For example, Kain says, "you read about kids who are outsiders, who get picked on, who have to use their wits to get out of bad situations, and you learn a little bit more about what it means to be a human being. You learn about what other people in your class might be going through."[55] Like books, video games show youth how it feels to be somebody else. Understanding how other people feel helps develop the important quality of empathy.

In addition to helping youth develop a better understanding of other people, some evidence shows that immersion in various video game stories can ultimately help young people learn to become better people. Jane McGonigal argues that games encourage players to be the best they can be. She says, "When we play a good game, we get to practice being the best version of ourselves: We become more optimistic, more creative, more focused, more likely to set ambitious goals, and more resilient in the face of failure."[56] A research study conducted at Stanford University suggests that when players pretend to be a superior version of themselves, their behavior may carry over into the real world. In the study, participants wore virtual-reality goggles and had to fly to deliver a life-saving shot of insulin to a child. Researchers found that those participants who pretended to be Superman (rather than simply flying in a helicopter), displayed higher empathy toward other people after the game.

Games and Gender Stereotypes

Unfortunately, video games are also highly effective at teaching youth some things that are not so beneficial. One of these is gender stereotypes. While there are exceptions, the majority of video games portray males as powerful and females as either helpless or highly sexualized. Some believe that this translates into youth's learning these stereotypes. Game player Inger Junge gives the example of the *Mario* games, which are extremely popular among youth. She says, "The Mario Series . . . have you rescuing Princess Peach from her many, varied captors." Junge explains why this is harmful. She says: "This is

Making Algebra Fun

All youth eventually have to learn algebra in school, but for many of them it is both difficult and uninteresting. A video game called *DragonBox* could help change that. It helps players learn algebra in a way that is both fun and easy. As players learn they are able to feed baby dragons and watch them grow. *Wired* contributor Jonathan H. Liu says, "Within a couple hours, most kids playing *DragonBox* will be able to start solving simple algebraic equations, and what's more, they'll be having fun and they may not even know they're learning algebra at first." He says that his five-year-old is able to play the game and loves it. At the Washington State Algebra Challenge in 2013, the potential of the game was showcased. Students who played *DragonBox* were able to master algebra in an average of only forty-one minutes. *Forbes* contributor Jordan Shapiro asks, "Why didn't this exist when I was a kid? I hated algebra. I was terrified of variables. I avoided it at all costs. Now," he says, "I find myself playing DragonBox for fun."

Jonathan H. Liu, "*DragonBox:* Algebra Beats *Angry Birds*," *Wired*, June 13, 2012. www.wired.com.

Jordan Shapiro, "It Only Takes About 42 Minutes to Learn Algebra with Video Games," *Forbes*, July 1, 2013. www.forbes.com.

problematic on two fronts. Firstly it propagates that women are helpless and in constant need of saving. . . . Secondly Princess Peach serves quite literally as a trophy for the completion of Mario's quest. She is ultimately just another object or reward for Mario to use."[57] Gamer Carolyn Petit talks about *Grand Theft Auto V*, another very popular game. She points out that women in this game are also portrayed in very negative ways. She says, "GTA V has little room for women except to portray them as strippers, prostitutes, long-suffering wives, humorless girlfriends and goofy, new-age feminists we're meant to laugh at."[58] The effect of continually seeing females in these types of roles is to teach youth that this is normal and desirable behavior when in fact this is not true.

Video Games in Schools

For better or for worse, the fact is that video games are being used more frequently for learning. Research shows that their use in schools is becoming increasingly common. For example, the Joan Ganz Cooney Center conducted a national survey of 505 teachers in the United States about the use of video games in the classroom. It found that 32 percent of those surveyed use games two to four days per week, and 18 percent use them every day. Gaming in the classroom has traditionally meant using games specifically designed for education; however, that is changing too. An increasing number of teachers are utilizing popular games like *Minecraft* as a teaching tool. *Wall Street Journal* writer Stephanie Banchero reports, "Scores of teachers nationwide are using games such as 'Angry Birds,' 'Minecraft,' 'SimCity' and 'World of Warcraft' to teach math, science, writing, teamwork and even compassion. In Chicago and New York, entire schools have been created that use the principles of game design in curriculum development."[59]

> "The opportunity to work with video games at school feels so much less like work that most students are compelled to eagerly participate."[60]
>
> —Brian Herrig and Greg Taranto, educators.

Many people are enthusiastic about the potential of games for education. In the Joan Ganz Cooney Center survey, researchers found that 70 percent of teachers believe that video games help increase student engagement and motivation, and only 10 percent reported negative experiences with students using games in the classroom. Educators Brian Herrig and Greg Taranto argue that when teachers base a lesson around video games, student engagement is almost guaranteed. They state, "The opportunity to work with video games at school feels so much less like work that most students are compelled to eagerly participate."[60] Lucas Gillispie is technology coordinator of Pender County Schools in coastal North Carolina, which use video games as part of their curriculum. He calls teaching through video games ninja teaching. "The academic stuff is there," he says. "But it is so subtly woven into the fun and engagement that they don't realize they are learning."[61]

Some schools are turning to video games as teaching tools. Even games such as World of Warcraft *have been used in math, science, and writing assignments. Pictured are characters from the game.*

Learning Problem Solving

Another advantage of using video games in schools is that they offer a solution to the problem of students simply memorizing information but not learning how to use it for critical thinking and problem solving. Some people believe that education, particularly in the United States, has become too focused on simple memorization. California high school teacher Ben Orlin illustrates the issue with one of his teaching experiences. He says that when he taught his first trigonometry class he questioned students about sine, an important trigonometric function used to solve equations. He asked, "'What's the sine of $\pi/2$? . . . 'One!' they replied in unison. 'We learned that last year.'" As a result, Orlin says, "I skipped ahead, later to realize that they didn't really know what 'sine' even meant. They'd simply memorized that fact."[62]

Orlin believes that such mindless memorization is too common. He argues that rather than simple memorization, math should ac-

Angry Birds

Shari Hiltbrand, a middle school teacher at Kinkaid School in Houston, Texas, uses the popular video game *Angry Birds* in her classroom to help students understand physics. In *Angry Birds* players slingshot birds into towers of various sizes in order to knock down the towers. The game involves physics because players are dealing with the arc of the birds through the air, their descent, and their collision with the towers. In order to knock down the towers and get to the next level, players must get the trajectory of the birds exactly right. Hiltbrand has her students play the game, then use it to study the physics concepts of motion, force, mass, speed, and velocity. She has found that *Angry Birds* greatly enhances her students' understanding of these often difficult topics. In their writing she says, there is "such amazing clarity and precision, I see a deeper understanding of physics." She believes this game gives her a powerful tool with which to both engage her students and help them become more informed, scientific thinkers.

Quoted in Stephanie Banchero, "Now Teachers Encourage Computer Games in Class," *Wall Street Journal,* October 8, 2013. www.wsj.com.

tually be a process of thoughtful exploration and logical discovery. However, he found that for many students, "Trigonometry was just a collection of non-rhyming lyrics to the lamest sing-along ever."[63] Using video games in school can help overcome this problem because it forces the exploration and discovery that Orlin tries to teach. In a video game a student cannot simply memorize facts; instead he or she must use those facts to be innovative and solve problems.

Regular Learning Is Unable to Compete

Video games do appear to be an effective way to engage students and encourage them to be problem solvers; however, there are critics of game-based learning. They argue that while video games are an excellent way to engage youth, games also make the regular classroom setting seem so much less interesting by comparison. This is a problem because teachers cannot compete with the excitement of a game, and they find it difficult to maintain students' attention. Technology instructor Gary Butcher explains, "Video games give them a rush of excitement, and before long plain old learning can't compete."[64] Many teachers echo the complaint that constant exposure to video games and other digital technology is affecting students' ability to focus in the classroom. Hope Molina-Porter is an English teacher at Troy High School in Fullerton, California. She has been teaching for fourteen years and says it has become harder to hold her students' attention. "I'm an entertainer. I have to do a song and dance to capture their attention,"[65] she says. In addition to making it difficult for youth to concentrate in the classroom, the constant excitement of game-based learning can actually harm students. Butcher explains how games put players in a state of constant arousal. He says, "When I watch students engaged in video games, they appear tense, as if they're perched to literally slay the dragon."[66] This constant state of tension can be extremely stressful for young people.

Critics also caution that while video games can be an effective teaching tool, teachers should be careful not to rely on them too much. It is important to remember that learning should involve many different types of experiences, not just those in front of a screen. For example, author Richard Louv stresses the importance of learning from nature, too. He says, "If we're going to have kids sitting in front of screens more, we have to make sure they also sit in front of streams more."[67]

"Video games give . . . [students] a rush of excitement, and before long plain old learning can't compete."[64]

—Gary Butcher, technology instructor.

Overall, it is clear that game play involves more than mere entertainment; many players are also learning a wide variety of skills and information. Despite critiques such as Louv's and Butcher's, society has increasingly moved to embrace video games as a fun and effective teaching tool.

Regulation of
Video Games

In 1992 the one-on-one tournament fighting game *Mortal Kombat* was released in arcades. At the time this game was one of the most violent that the public had ever seen. Game writer Joseph Stillwell describes it. He says, "Just about every hit that connected during a round of Mortal Kombat caused massive amounts of blood to splatter all over the screen. One character could throw a harpoon into his opponent's neck."[68] Stillwell says that this was considered to be pretty gruesome then. Yet the constant blood and violence was not the most shocking part of the game. Stillwell says, "What really caused most of the controversy was the game's 'fatalities,' brutal finishing moves that allowed players to do things like decapitate their opponents, rip out their hearts, or burn them alive."[69] This level of violence shocked and outraged many people, and they worried that it would be particularly harmful for youth. The response to *Mortal Kombat* and other early games with extreme violence or highly sexual content was a push for regulation.

These games spurred a history of repeated attempts at government regulation of video games, attempts that continue to this day. Critics continue to insist that youth in the United States are being exposed to game content that is inappropriate and harmful for them and that they need to be protected through government regulation. On the other side, opponents of regulation argue that it is both unnecessary and unconstitutional. Thus far, all attempts at government regulation have failed; however, the debate resurfaces every few years when another politician or state government attempts to pass a new game regulation measure.

Entertainment Software Rating Board

While the video game industry is not regulated by the government, it is not without regulation. In response to the outcry over *Mortal*

Kombat and other games in the early 1990s, the video game industry created its own system of regulation. The Entertainment Software Rating Board (ESRB) was created in 1994. This nonprofit organization assigns ratings and enforces industry-adopted guidelines for game advertising. In the United States, almost every game sold in a retail store has been rated by the ESRB. Ratings have three parts. One is the category: Early Childhood (C), Everyone (E), Everyone 10+ (E 10+), Teen (T) for ages 13 and up, Mature (M) for ages 17 and up, and Adult (A) for ages 18 and up. Game labels also contain descriptions that explain in more detail why a game has been given a particular rating. For instance, some games might carry this explanation: "Blood and Gore—Depictions of blood or the mutilation of body parts." Others might have this description: "Strong Sexual Content—Explicit and/or frequent depictions of sexual behavior, possibly including nudity." Finally, ratings include information about the interactive elements of a game such as whether the game shares the user's location with other users. Digitally distributed games are not subject to the same requirements or enforcement as packaged or boxed games; however, the ESRB strongly encourages their makers to follow its guidelines.

"What really caused most of the controversy was the [*Mortal Kombat*] game's 'fatalities,' brutal finishing moves that allowed players to do things like decapitate their opponents, rip out their hearts, or burn them alive."[69]

—Joseph Stillwell, a journalist who writes about video games.

ESRB Success

Many people believe the ESRB does a good job of accurately rating games and informing players and parents about content. Research conducted in 2012 by Peter D. Hart Research Associates found that 85 percent of parents are aware of the ESRB rating system, and 88 percent believe it is either "very helpful" or "somewhat helpful" in helping them choose games for their children. Researcher Christopher Clements calls the ESRB rating system "the lone bright spot" in the controversy over video game regulation. He says, "The ESRB has a proven, successful method of screening and rating video games for explicit content, which educates parents that purchase these games."[70] D. Ryan Johnson is one parent who praises the ESRB system. In a comment to an online article about violent video games he says, "I feel that the rating system for games is a really good guide for parents who do not know games, and I follow and plan to continue to follow its suggestions with my kids." He adds, "The rating is always on the front. It's easier than even movies!"[71]

Some evidence supports the idea that retailers also do a good job of helping the regulatory system work by enforcing age-based ratings for video games. The Federal Trade Commission (FTC) regularly conducts undercover investigations of the video game and other entertainment industries to see how well ratings are enforced. In these investigations youth unaccompanied by a parent attempt to purchase video games that are rated M (meaning for players aged seventeen or older), R-rated movie tickets, R-rated DVDs, or music CDs with a parental advisory label warning of explicit content. In their latest study—conducted in 2012—they found that only 13 percent of underage shoppers were able to buy M-rated video games. This is the same percentage as in 2010.

It is also the highest level of compliance among the video game, music, and movie industries, showing that of the three, the video

The video game industry ratings system helps consumers determine which content is suitable for various ages. Games with the E10+ rating (for ages ten and older) may contain cartoon violence, mild language, and/or minimally suggestive themes.

54

game industry is doing the best job of keeping youth from purchasing games intended for adults. In the 2012 FTC study, 30 percent of underage shoppers were able to buy R-rated DVDs, 24 percent purchased R-rated movie tickets, and 47 percent were able to buy music CDs with a parental advisory label.

Critiques of the Ratings System

However, despite the high level of praise for the ESRB, there is still extensive disagreement on whether this voluntary system of regulation is enough. Critics argue that despite industry self-regulation, large numbers of youth play video games containing mature content that is not appropriate for them. They insist that there needs to be additional regulation of video games in order to protect these youth. Former US representative from California Joe Baca insists that the entertainment industry has failed to live up to its responsibility to adequately inform consumers about their products. He says, "The video game industry has a responsibility to parents, families and to consumers—to inform them of the potentially damaging content that is often found in their products." However, Baca says, "they have repeatedly failed to live up to this responsibility."[72] In 2012 he introduced a bill in the US House of Representatives that would have required most video games to include a warning label about the potential harms of violent content. The label would have stated, "Exposure to violent video games has been linked to aggressive behavior."[73] The bill failed to pass.

> "The video game industry has a responsibility to parents, families and to consumers— to inform them of the potentially damaging content that is often found in their products."[72]
>
> —Joe Baca, former US representative from California.

The Role of Parents

One problem preventing video game regulation is that it is unclear whether increased regulation would actually achieve the goal of protecting children from games with violent and mature content. Research shows that while large numbers of youth do play games with high levels of violence and other mature content, this is not because of a lack of ratings or ratings enforcement. In fact, the research shows that information about content is prominently displayed on games, and most retailers do not sell M-rated games to youth. Instead, many youth play these games because their parents allow it. In an article for the *Boston College Law Review*, Clements investigates the role of parents. He says, "Curiously, studies by the Federal Trade Commission (FTC) and the ESRB reported that eighty-nine percent of parents are involved in the purchase of a video game for their child and, seventy-five percent of parents regularly check the rating of a video game before purchasing it. In addition, the most recent FTC mystery shopper study found that eighty percent of individuals under seventeen were turned away by retailers when attempting to purchase an M-rated video game." Clements says, "Taken together, these studies paint a curious picture of children playing games deemed inappropriate for their age purchased predominantly by their own parents."[74] He concludes that the only way for legislators to keep violent games away from children would be to completely ban them.

One video game store employee has been working in video game retail for almost ten years and routinely sees parents buying M-rated games for their children, even after being explicitly told about the mature content of these games. This employee talks about *Grand Theft Auto V* (rated M, for age seventeen and older), and says that many parents buy this game for their young children, even after they have been warned about it. The employee says he tells parents, "[This game has] a first-person view of half-naked strippers or that the game has a mission that forces you to torture another human being." The employee adds, "Last week my store sold over a thousand copies of *GTA V*, at least a hundred of which were sold to parents for children who could barely even see over my counter."[75]

> "It has, if anything, become more important to supplement parents' authority to guide their children's development."[76]
>
> —Stephen Breyer, justice of the US Supreme Court.

The parents allowing their children to play mature video games do so for different reasons. Some are simply too busy to be involved

56

Making Money from Game Players

While much of the controversy over regulation centers on protecting youth from video game content that might be harmful—such as violent or sexual content—some people believe young game players need another type of protection. When they play games online, many youth are unknowingly being studied by marketing researchers. These researchers track and analyze the way people play in order to understand how they can make money from players by making them spend money inside games. For example, in *Call of Duty* players can buy a new gun, or in *FarmVille* they can buy a cow. Journalist Steve Henn explains how researchers manipulate people into spending money on games. He says, "The idea is to make gamers uncomfortable, frustrate them, take away their powers, crush their forts—and then, at the last second, offer them a way out for a price." Adults are old enough to understand that such manipulation occurs and that they consent to it when they decide to play a game. However, critics wonder whether there should be some kind of regulation to protect youth who may be too young to give their informed consent for such practices.

Steve Henn, "How Video Games Are Getting Inside Your Head—and Wallet," *NPR*, October 29, 2013. www.npr.org.

in their children's game play and they allow access to mature games without truly understanding what their children are doing. Proponents of regulation argue that because parents are so busy, they need increased regulation to help them monitor their children's media use. Data show that the number of unmonitored children may be substantial. Supreme Court justice Stephen Breyer says, "Today, 5.3 million grade-school-age children of working parents are routinely home alone. . . . Thus, it has, if anything, become more important to supplement parents' authority to guide their children's development."[76] Yet other parents purposely allow their children access to mature games, arguing that such exposure is inevitable anyway and that by allowing it, parents can also help their children learn to deal with it. Video game player "Kevin M" says, "They will be exposed to these things one way or another, I know my parents sitting me down and always emphasizing that the games I was playing were just pretend. It gave me perspective."[77]

The First Amendment

One reason video game regulation remains unsuccessful is the existence of the First Amendment to the US Constitution. The amendment states, "Congress shall make no law . . . abridging the freedom of speech." This means that individuals have the right to express themselves without interference or restriction from the government, even if some people find that expression offensive or inappropriate. This includes expression through art and entertainment, including movies, books, and video games. The Media Coalition explains that because of the First Amendment, any government action to restrict speech must be for an extremely good reason. It says, "To warrant abridging our cherished Constitutional freedoms of speech and expression, the dangers of that content must be immediate and grave, the evidence must be incontrovertible and a no-less-severe alternative to censoring the speech can exist."[78]

In a small number of circumstances the courts have decided that certain types of expression do warrant government restriction. In these cases it has been decided that a restriction of that expression is necessary for the protection of the public. For example, the First Amendment does not protect the right to yell "Fire!" in a crowded theater because to do so would create a real possibility of injury. Likewise, obscenity is restricted because the courts have determined that there is a real danger of youth being harmed by exposure to it. Some people argue that like obscenity, video games with extremely violent or sexual content are a serious threat to youth, and this justifies their restriction.

Court Rulings

There have been numerous attempts in the United States to restrict video game content in the name of protecting youth. However, all have been struck down by the courts as unconstitutional. Most recently, in 2011 the US Supreme Court struck down a California law that would have prohibited retailers from selling M-rated games to minors. Retailers found breaking the law would have subjected them to a $1,000 fine.

Parents often allow their children to buy games intended for more mature players. Some parents do not understand the games their kids play while others do not have a problem with their kids playing these games.

Fear of New Forms of Media

Video games are a relatively new form of media, and history shows that new media are often feared by the public and subject to criticism and calls for regulation. History also shows that fears about the corruption of youth by new media have frequently proved to be unfounded. For example, in 1982 *Ms. Pacman* was released in arcades and spurred widespread criticism. A rabbi warned on television that video games like this were teaching youth to see other people as "blips to be destroyed." US surgeon general C. Everett Koop warned that video games were one of the main causes of family violence. Today such warnings seem greatly exaggerated. Overall, the *Economist* says, "there is a long tradition of dire warning about new forms of media, from translations of the Bible in vernacular languages to cinema and rock music." However, it says, "As time passes such novelties become uncontroversial, and eventually some are elevated into art forms."

Economist, "No Killer App; the Moral Panic About Video Games Is Subsiding," December 10, 2011. www.economist.com.

In its ruling the court stresses that the First Amendment protects video games, even if their content is objectionable to some people. It says, "Like the protected books, plays, and movies that preceded them, video games communicate ideas—and even social messages—through many familiar literary devices (such as characters, dialogue, plot, and music) and through features distinctive to the medium (such as the player's interaction with the virtual world). That suffices to confer First Amendment protection."[79] It insists that the government has no power to make moral or aesthetic judgments about art and literature, including video games, even if the majority of the population agrees. Instead, the First Amendment guarantees that individuals have the freedom to express themselves through such content, and other individuals have the freedom to choose whether to view or listen to that content. The court points out that video game regulation would take away that freedom. Game regulation, it says, "abridges the First Amendment rights of young people whose parents (and aunts and uncles) think violent video games are a harmless pastime."[80]

In addition to leaving choices about game consumption in the hands of individuals rather than the government, the expression of various ideas through video games serves another important role in society. It exposes people to ideas and experiences that are different from their own, broadening their understanding and giving them the information they need to make their own decisions about various issues. Game designer Randy Pitchford talks about the value of violent games in particular. He argues that violence is a function of the human condition and it is better for society to examine it and decide how to deal with it rather than simply ignore its existence. He says, "Considering violence and its manifestations in media is extremely helpful and useful for us. Our species becomes better, stronger and less violent through the thoughtful examination of violence and its consequences."[81] Pitchford argues that games are an ideal way to examine violence because they replicate it without actually harming anybody.

> "[Game regulation] abridges the First Amendment rights of young people whose parents (and aunts and uncles) think violent video games are a harmless pastime."[80]
>
> —US Supreme Court ruling, 2011

Future Attempts at Regulation Are Likely

Yet not everybody agrees with the idea that video games should be free from all regulation. In the 2011 Supreme Court case Justice Samuel Alito states that some type of video game regulation might be justified. He argues that while the First Amendment does indeed protect many forms of entertainment such as movies and books, there is reason to believe that video games are potentially more harmful to youth than these other types of media. For example, many games are highly realistic and interactive. He says, "When all of the characteristics of video games are taken into account, there is certainly a reasonable basis for thinking that the experience of playing a video game may be quite different from the experience of reading a book, listening to a radio broadcast, or viewing a movie." As a result, he argues, "I would not squelch legislative efforts to deal with what is perceived by some to be a significant and developing social problem."[82]

Based on the history of the video game controversy, future legislative efforts are likely. The 2011 court case was only one of many attempts that have been made to regulate games. According to the ESA, thus far a total of thirteen different court rulings state that video games and computer games are protected speech and that legislative bodies cannot ban or limit access to them without violating the First Amendment.

Source Notes

Introduction: A Favorite Pastime

1. Steve Henn, "How Video Games Are Getting Inside Your Head—and Wallet," NPR, October 29, 2013. www.npr.org.
2. Quoted in Henn, "How Video Games Are Getting Inside Your Head—and Wallet."
3. Jane McGonigal, "Video Games: An Hour a Day Is Key to Success in Life," *Huffington Post*, February 15, 2011. www.huffington post.com.
4. American Academy of Child & Adolescent Psychiatry, "Children and Video Games: Playing with Violence," *Facts for Families*, March 2011. www.aacap.org.
5. Isabela Granic, Adam Lobel, and Rutger C.M.E. Engels, "The Benefits of Playing Video Games," *American Psychologist*, January 2014, p. 70.
6. James Paul Gee and Elisabeth R. Hayes, *Women and Gaming: The Sims and 21st Century Learning*. New York: Palgrave Macmillan, 2010, pp. 27–28.

Chapter One: Video Games Research

7. Shankar Vedantam, "It's a Duel: How Do Violent Video Games Affect Kids?," NPR, July 7, 2011. www.npr.org.
8. Quoted in Vedantam, "It's a Duel."
9. Quoted in Vedantam, "It's a Duel."
10. Isabela Granic, Adam Lobel, and Rutger C.M.E. Engels, "The Benefits of Playing Video Games," p. 74.
11. Quoted in Jason Schreier, "From Halo to Hot Sauce: What 25 Years of Violent Video Game Research Looks Like," Kotaku, January 17, 2013. http://kotaku.com.

12. Media Coalition, "Only a Game: Why Censoring New Media Won't Stop Gun Violence," 2013. www.mediacoalition.org.
13. Craig A. Anderson, Douglas A. Gentile, and Karen E. Dill, "Chapter 13: Prosocial, Antisocial, and Other Effects of Recreational Video Games," in D.G. Singer and J.L. Singer, eds., *Handbook of Children and the Media*, 2nd ed. Thousand Oaks, CA: Sage, 2012, p. 257.
14. Christopher J. Ferguson and John Kilburn, "The Public Health Risks of Media Violence: A Meta-Analytic Review," *Journal of Pediatrics*, February 23, 2009. www.jpeds.com.
15. Barack Obama, "Remarks by the President and the Vice President on Gun Violence," January 16, 2013. www.whitehouse .gov.

Chapter Two: Violent Game Play

16. Quoted in Euronews, "Columbine Marks Tragic Anniversary," April 20, 2013. www.euronews.com.
17. Samuel Alito, opinion, U.S. Supreme Court, *Brown, Governor of California, et al. v. Entertainment Merchants Association et al.*, June 27, 2011.
18. "ir1449," "DayZ Is a Murder Simulator Like No Other," Reddit, January 2014. www.reddit.com.
19. Quoted in Vedantam, "It's a Duel."
20. Craig A. Anderson and Wayne A. Warburton, "The Impact of Violent Video Games: An Overview," in Wayne Warburton and Danya Braunstein, eds., *Growing Up Fast and Furious: Reviewing the Impacts of Violent and Sexualised Media on Children*. Annandale, NSW, Australia: Federation, 2012, p. 72.
21. Scott Shackford, "Imaginary Guns Don't Kill People, Either," *American Spectator*, November 2013. http://spectator.org.
22. Quoted in Jim Avila, "School Shooter: 'I Didn't Realize' They Would Die," ABC News, June 11, 2008. http://abcnews.go.com.
23. Anderson and Warburton, "The Impact of Violent Video Games: An Overview," p. 71.
24. Brad Bushman, interviewed by Jeffrey Brown, "Can Violent Games Play a Role in Violent Behavior?," PBS, February 19, 2013. www.pbs.org.

25. Quoted in John Gaudiosi, "Norway Suspect Used Call of Duty to Train for Massacre," *Forbes*, July 24, 2011. www.forbes.com.

26. Robert VerBruggen, "The Folly of Blaming Video Games," *National Review*, December 20, 2012. www.nationalreview.com.

27. Aaron Sampson, "In Defense of Video Game Violence: A Personal Account of the Impact of Gaming, Gun Ownership, and Growing Up," Gamespot, February 7, 2013. www.gamespot.com.

28. Michael Venables, "Violence in Video Games: It's All Part of Growing Up," *Wired*, September 6, 2011. www.wired.com.

29. Gee and Hayes, *Women and Gaming*, p. 27.

30. Cheryl K. Olson, "It's Perverse, but It's Also Pretend," *New York Times*, June 27, 2011. www.nytimes.com.

31. Paul Tassi, "The Idiocy of Blaming Video Games for the Norway Massacre," *Forbes*, April 19, 2012. www.forbes.com.

32. Quoted in David Edwards, "Former FBI Profiler: 'Video Games Do Not Cause Violence,'" Raw Story, February 24, 2013. www.rawstory.com.

Chapter Three: Video Games and Health

33. Quoted in Tracy Miller, "Can Video Games Fight Cancer? Re-Mission 2 Aims to Give Young Patients a Fun Way to Battle Their Serious Diseases," *New York Daily News*, May 6, 2013. www.nydailynews.com.

34. Maia Szalavitz, "Study: Playing a Video Game Helps Teens Beat Depression," *Time*, April 20, 2012. www.time.com.

35. Daniel Johnson, Christian Jones, and Jane Burns, "Beyond the Beat-Em-Up: Video Games Are Good for Young People," The Conversation, August 30, 2013. http://theconversation.com.

36. Quoted in Science Daily, "Risks, Consequences of Video Game Addiction Identified in New Study," January 19, 2011. www.sciencedaily.com.

37. Liz Woolley, interviewed by TFP Student Action, "How Video Games Kill the Body and Soul," July 9, 2012. www.tfpstudentaction.org.

38. Woolley, interview, "How Video Games Kill the Body and Soul."

39. Quoted in NPR Staff, "When Playing Video Games Means Sitting on Life's Sidelines," NPR, October 20, 2013. www.npr.org.

40. American Psychiatric Association, "Internet Gaming Disorder," *DSM-5 Development*, May 2013. www.dsm5.org.

41. Video Game Addiction, "Social Consequences of Gaming Addiction." www.video-game-addiction.org.

42. Cheryl K. Olson, "Children's Motivations for Video Game Play in the Context of Normal Development," *Review of General Psychology*, 2010. www.apa.org.

43. Jane McGonigal, *Reality Is Broken: Why Games Make Us Better and How They Can Change the World*. New York: Penguin, 2011, p. 93.

44. American Heart Association, "Overweight in Children," January 28, 2014. www.heart.org.

45. Matthew Cod, "Just Dance 2014," NZ Gamer, October 10, 2013. http://nzgamer.com.

46. Tom Baranowski et al., "Impact of an Active Video Game on Healthy Children's Physical Activity," *Pediatrics*, February 27, 2012. http://pediatrics.aappublications.org.

47. Anderson and Warburton, "The Impact of Violent Video Games: An Overview," p. 78.

Chapter Four: Games and Learning

48. Peter Tromba, "Build Engagement and Knowledge One Block at a Time with Minecraft," *Learning and Leading with Technology*, June/July 2013. www.iste.org.

49. James Paul Gee, "Foreword," in Constance Steinkuehler, Kurt Squire, and Sasha Barab, *Games, Learning, and Society: Learning and Meaning in the Digital Age*. New York: Cambridge University Press, 2012, p. xvii.

50. Quoted in Greg Toppo, "White House Office Studies Benefits of Video Games," *USA Today*, February 2, 2012. www.usatoday.com.

51. Toppo, "White House Office Studies Benefits of Video Games."

52. Isabela Granic, Adam Lobel, and Rutger C.M.E. Engels, "The Benefits of Playing Video Games," *American Psychologist*, January 2014, p. 68.

53. Granic, Lobel, and Engels, "The Benefits of Playing Video Games," p. 73.

54. Anonymous, reply to "Are There Any Games to Help My 9 Year Old Son with Autism to gain Confidence?," blog, *Quibly*, February 6, 2014. http://quib.ly/blog.

55. Erik Kain, "Virtually Crime Free: How Video Games May Help Prevent Crime," *Forbes*, August 10, 2011. www.forbes.com.

56. McGonigal, "Video Games: An Hour a Day Is Key to Success in Life."

57. Inger Junge, "Women Not Allowed in Techno-Geek & Gaming Culture," Sister Namibia, June 2013. www.sisternamibia.org.

58. Carolyn Petit, *Grand Theft Auto V* review, "City of Angels and Demons," Gamespot. www.gamespot.com.

59. Stephanie Banchero, "Now Teachers Encourage Computer Games in Class," *Wall Street Journal*, October 8, 2013. www.wsj .com.

60. Brian Herrig and Greg Taranto, "Being a Game Changer," *Technology and Engineering Teacher*, November 2012, p. 31.

61. Quoted in Banchero, "Now Teachers Encourage Computer Games in Class."

62. Ben Orlin, "When Memorization Gets in the Way of Learning," *Atlantic*, September 9, 2013. www.theatlantic.com.

63. Orlin, "When Memorization Gets in the Way of Learning."

64. Gary Butcher and Kyle Dunbar, "Video Games: Helpful or Harmful?," *Learning & Leading with Technology*, May 2012. www .iste.org.

65. Quoted in Matt Richtell, "Technology Changing How Students Learn, Teachers Say," *New York Times*, November 1, 2012. www .nytimes.com.

66. Butcher and Dunbar, "Video Games: Helpful or Harmful?"

67. Quoted in Greg Toppo, "Video Game Invades Classroom, Scores Education Points," *USA Today*, March 4, 2013. www.usatoday .com.

Chapter Five: Regulation of Video Games

68. Joseph Stillwell, "The Original Mortal Kombat Controversy," *USBLAWG*, October 18, 2013. www.usblawg.com.

69. Stillwell, "The Original Mortal Kombat Controversy."

70. Christopher Clements, "Protecting Protected Speech: Violent Game Legislation Post–*Brown v. Entertainment Merchants Ass'n*," *Boston College Law Review*, 2012. http://lawdigitalcommons.bc.edu.

71. D. Ryan Johnson, comment on "10 Violent Video Games to Avoid," *Parenting*, January 6, 2013. www.parenting.com.

72. Quoted in Pete Kasperowicz, "House Members Call for New Labels Warning Against 'Violent' Video Games," *The Hill*, March 20, 2012. www.thehill.com.

73. H.R. 4204. www.govtrack.us.

74. Clements, "Protecting Protected Speech."

75. Your Average Video Game Retail Veteran, "I Sold Too Many Copies of *GTA V* to Parents Who Didn't Give a Damn," Kotaku, September 23, 2013. http://kotaku.com.

76. Stephen Breyer, dissenting opinion, U.S. Supreme Court, *Brown, Governor of California, et al. v. Entertainment Merchants Association et al.* June 27, 2011.

77. Kevin M, comment to Vedantam, "It's a Duel: How Do Violent Video Games Affect Kids?," NPR, July 7, 2011. www.npr.org.

78. Media Coalition, "Only a Game: Why Censoring New media Won't Stop Gun Violence," 2013. www.mediacoalition.org.

79. Antonin Scalia, majority opinion, U.S. Supreme Court, *Brown, Governor of California, et al. v. Entertainment Merchants Association et al.* June 27, 2011.

80. Scalia, majority opinion, U.S. Supreme Court, *Brown, Governor of California, et al. v. Entertainment Merchants Association et al.*

81. Randy Pitchford, answer to "Point . . . Counterpoint: Do Videogames Inspire Violent Behavior? Absolutely *Not* Says Vidgame Developer Randy Pitchford. Absolutely *Yes*, Says Lt. Col. David Grossman," *Variety*, 2012. www.variety.com.

82. Samuel Alito, opinion, U.S. Supreme Court, *Brown, Governor of California, et al. v. Entertainment Merchants Association et al.* June 27, 2011.

Center for Successful Parenting

PO Box 3794
Carmel, IN 46082
e-mail: csp@onrampamerica.net
website: www.sosparents.org

The Center for Successful Parenting believes that violent video games are harmful to the development of children. Its website contains news and research about the effects of video games.

Common Sense Media

650 Townsend St., Suite 435
San Francisco, CA 94103
phone: (415) 863-0600 • fax: (415) 863-0601
website: www.commonsensemedia.org

Common Sense Media is a nonprofit organization that works to provide trustworthy information about media to youth and families. It believes families should have an informed choice about the media they consume. Its website has video game reviews and research.

Entertainment Consumers Association (ECA)

64 Danbury Rd., Suite 700
Wilton, CT 06897
phone: (203) 761-6180 • fax: (203) 761-6184
e-mail: feedback@theeca.com
website: www.theeca.com

The ECA is a nonprofit organization that represents video game players. It is opposed to the regulation of video games based on content and supports the current system of self-regulation by the game industry. Its website contains facts and position papers about video games.

Entertainment Software Association (ESA)

575 7th St. NW, Suite 300
Washington, DC 20004
website: www.theesa.com

The ESA is the trade association for the US computer game and video game industry. Its website contains numerous research reports and facts and articles about video games.

Entertainment Software Rating Board (ESRB)

317 Madison Ave., 22nd Floor
New York, NY 10017
phone: (212) 759-0700
website: www.esrb.org

The ESRB is the nonprofit, self-regulatory body that assigns ratings for video games and apps so parents can make informed choices. Its website has information about the video game rating system and its enforcement.

International Game Developers Association (IGDA)

19 Mantua Rd.
Mount Royal, NJ 08061
phone: (856) 423-2990 • fax: (856) 423-3420
e-mail: contact@igda.org
website: www.igda.org

The IGDA is an industry association that promotes the interests of the people who create video games. It is opposed to censorship of games. Its website contains articles and reports about video games.

Media Smarts

950 Gladstone Ave., Suite 120
Ottawa, ON
K1Y 3E6 Canada
phone: (613) 224-7721 • fax: (613) 761-9024
e-mail: info@mediasmarts.ca
website: http://mediasmarts.ca

Media Smarts is a Canadian organization that works to educate young people so that they can develop critical thinking skills and be informed media users. Its website contains news, research, and articles about video games.

Parent Further

615 First Ave. NE, Suite 125
Minneapolis, MN 55413
phone: (800) 888-7828
e-mail: info@parentfurther.com
website: www.parentfurther.com

Parent Further provides research and education about the impact of video games on youth and families. Its website provides reviews of video games in addition to fact sheets and articles about their effects.

For Further Research

Books

Simon Egenfeldt-Nielsen, Jonas Heide Smith, and Susana Pajares Tosca, *Understanding Video Games: The Essential Introduction*. New York: Routledge, 2013.

Devin C. Griffiths, *Virtual Ascendance: Video Games and the Remaking of Reality*. Lanham, MD: Rowman & Littlefield, 2013.

Steven J. Kirsh, *Children, Adolescents, and Media Violence: A Critical Look at the Research*. Thousand Oaks, CA: Sage, 2012.

Scott Rigby and Richard M. Ryan, *Glued to Games: How Video Games Draw Us In and Hold Us Spellbound*. Santa Barbara, CA: Praeger, 2011.

Dorothy G. Singer and Jerome L. Singer, *Handbook of Children and the Media*. 2nd ed. Thousand Oaks, CA: Sage, 2011.

Constance Steinkuehler, Kurt Squire, and Sasha Barab, *Games, Learning, and Society: Learning and Meaning in the Digital Age*. New York: Cambridge University Press, 2012.

Internet Sources

Stephanie Banchero, "Now Teachers Encourage Computer Games in Class," *Wall Street Journal*, October 8, 2013. http://online.wsj.com/news/articles/SB10001424127887324665604579081030943142894.

Christopher Clements, "Protecting Protected Speech: Violent Game Legislation Post–*Brown v. Entertainment Merchants Ass'n*," *Boston College Law Review*, 2012. http://lawdigitalcommons.bc.edu/cgi/view content.cgi?article=3217&context=bclr.

Entertainment Software Association, "Essential Facts About the Computer and Video Game Industry," 2013. www.theesa.com/facts/pdfs/esa_ef_2013.pdf.

Isabela Granic, Adam Lobel, and Rutger C.M.E. Engels, "The Benefits of Playing Video Games," *American Psychologist*, January 2014. www.apa.org/pubs/journals/releases/amp-a0034857.pdf.

Steve Henn, "How Video Games Are Getting Inside Your Head—and Wallet," NPR, October 29, 2013. www.npr.org/blogs/alltech considered/2013/10/30/241449067/how-video-games-are-getting -inside-your-head-and-wallet.

Michael Venables, "Violence in Video Games: It's All Part of Growing Up," *Wired*, September 6, 2011. www.wired.com/geekdad/2011/09 /violence.

Index

About the Author

Andrea C. Nakaya, a native of New Zealand, holds a BA in English and an MA in communications from San Diego State University. She has written and edited more than thirty books on current issues. She currently lives in Encinitas, California, with her husband and their two children, Natalie and Shane.